THESE TREES

THESE TREES

Ruthie Rosauer

★ ★ ROSE RIVER PRESS ★ ★

THESE TREES

by Ruthie Rosauer

Rose River Press

Copyright © 2017 by Rose River Press

Rose River Press
P.O. Box 6011
Hendersonville, NC 28793
www.RoseRiverPress.com

Library of Congress Control Number:
2017938508

ISBN: 978-0-9986245-0-1

*The paper used in this publication is SFI
(Sustainable Forestry Initiative) certified sustainable.*

Printed in U.S.A.
Edited by Ruth Rosauer
Design and Layout by Gary Perrone

All photographs by Ruthie Rosauer
www.RuthieRosePhotography.com

This book is dedicated to my husband, Mark Rosauer,
without whose unfailing love, patience and support this book
would never have become a reality.

These Trees

by Carol Pearce Bjorlie

These trees were not destined for church bulletins
dyed purple for Lent
geology textbooks, rafts, campfires or violins.

They were here for the squirrel family,
avian choir, rope swing.

These green gods with their thousand eyes,
breathed their green breath over us
then dazzled with brilliant fire.

Winter branches tore into clouds
disappeared into snow in the white storm.

They teach us perseverance.

Table of Contents

Preface

I photograph trees because I love them. I do not consider myself to be an 'artistic' person – if I drew a horse and a dog I would have to label them so you would know which was which. I would never attempt to draw or paint a tree. But, like most people, I have taken photographs when on vacation. And I have been privileged to visit some very beautiful places with interesting trees such as Olympic National Park, the Bois de Boulogne in Paris, Longwood Gardens in Pennsylvania and the National Tropical Botanical Garden in Kauai.

I don't remember ever consciously setting out to photograph trees. But, "beauty is in the eye of the beholder," as the old adage says, and soon my friends and family began to notice that my vacation scrapbooks were lopsided with a preponderance of trees. I remember well a time when I was visiting Paris with my girlfriend, Liz. I was blissfully absorbed in photographing the bark of a tree. After a long interval of foot tapping Liz finally interrupted me, 'Will you just turn around and look at this view?' She was pointing to the Eiffel Tower. Which I duly admired for a minute, snapped the shutter once in its direction, and then went back to circling the tree.

"Those who dwell among the beauties and mysteries of the earth are never alone or weary of life."
– *Rachel Carson*

Photographing a tree is the closest I can come to sending a valentine to that tree; it is an outlet for my admiration and awe. Occasionally I am so moved by a tree that I do, literally, drop to my knees in reverence. I doubt that the tree is aware of my feelings. But in expressing them I hope to open myself to receiving something I cannot define from the tree. It is my attempt to signal to the tree, "I am here and I am paying attention."

A friend of mine whose spouse is a devoted shutterbug said to me in frustration, "Why can't he just enjoy looking at a flower or an elk without having to stand around and take a picture of it?" As much as I value my friendship with her, and knew it was my duty as a friend to cluck sympathetically, I couldn't take her side on this one! I knew exactly what her husband was going through. For me, taking a picture of something is how I 'enjoy' looking at it.

Taking a picture of a tree is the best way I know of to focus my attention exclusively on that tree. I'm not thinking about where we might go to lunch later, or whether Kevin has answered my email. Looking through the viewfinder limits not only my vision, but also my mind, to the subject I have chosen for my focus.

In this day and age, where we scroll through Facebook posts as we watch television, and check our emails while we talk on our cell phones, taking a photograph of a tree fills my hands with a camera, my mind on composing the shot, and my vision with the area framed by the viewfinder. I have room for nothing else while I am photographing a tree. This is no small gift in the 21 st century.

"And you will know exactly who you are,
forever, by knowing what it is that you love."

– Mark Helprin

My adoration of trees has spurred my willingness to upgrade the quality of my camera and to learn how to use it better. I started with a 'point and shoot' and now use a Sony RX10. I used to think tripods were too cumbersome. But after shooting hundreds of pictures that turned out to be a little blurry, I have finally conceded that a tripod is indispensable. Now I feel reckless when I take a picture without one. Here is a photography tip from me: You are just kidding yourself if you think you don't need a tripod!

As I said before, I photograph trees because I love them. I photographed them for many years without any thought towards sharing them with anyone else. I first shared my photographs to the general public on a website I created for a book I co-authored with Liz Hill in 2009 (www.Singingmeditation.com).

A few years later I entered some photos in an art show at Tryon Painters and Sculptors in Tryon, NC and received positive feedback (thank you Aviva Kahn). Since 2013 I have been exhibiting photographs in shows and galleries in western North Carolina.

I created this book so that I could share with you the wonder and beauty of trees I have been privileged to visit. A few years ago this planet had slightly more than three trillion trees. 15.3 million of them are logged each year to clear more land for agricultural and residential uses, as well as those 'harvested' for wood products – paper, construction, containers, furniture, etc. And that's not counting the millions of trees lost to wildfire (not beneficial controlled burns). It is estimated there will be no rainforests left in 100 years.

Poems are placed near some of the photographs. The choice of poems to pair with photographs was based on whether there was something in one that echoed, enhanced, or corresponded with the other. I had considered making a book of photographs without any text because I thought words would be distracting. Then I saw a book that contained only photographs. The photography was superb, but I felt 'lonely' leafing through it. One of the functions of the poems, I hope, is to be a friendly 'fellow traveler' in this world of beauty; not to intrude upon your solitude, but to share it with you.

An "About the Poets" section follows the main body of the book. It includes a brief biographical statement from each poet, an attribution for the poem if it has been previously published, and the poet's website if she or he has one.

In the "About the Trees" section there is a thumbnail photo of a tree, the page number where the larger photo appears in this book, its name (nearly all *are* given as "common names" rather than the Latin "scientific names" because that is how I know them), its native region and the location where I photographed the particular tree.

Frank Sinatra sings that his regrets are 'too few to mention.' Sadly, my regrets in editing this book are large enough to mention. My biggest one is that I cannot identify each and every tree on these pages. When I started photographing trees I did so as a way to capture a bit of their grandeur and artistry so I could revisit their memory when I was far away. So in the beginning, even when a botanical garden or arboretum helpfully provided name tags I did not make note of the names. After all, my goal was to preserve beauty – not be bogged down in what I then thought of as superfluous details.

Later, when I did have a glimmer of a thought to create this book, I did try to keep track of the signs placed near a tree. Unfortunately, not all the information I preserved was correct. As I endeavored to confirm tree identification with books and online sources in preparation for this book I found some of the tree names I had painstakingly preserved did not correspond to the pictures in front of me. Perhaps I noted down the tag of the plant in front of the tree, or of the tree beside the tree of interest. And I photographed plenty of trees that had no tags whatsoever!

For tree identification after the fact I enlisted the help of a retired forester, a botanist and anyone else who I thought was knowledgeable. Even so, there are still some trees whose identities elude me. All errors in tree identification reside with me. I hope that the lack of identification will not subtract from the Reader's appreciation for the beauty of the trees.

My hope for this book

Some scientists now believe that even looking at pictures of trees can lower heart rates and stress levels. That might be one by-product of looking at this book. But my foremost hope is that by turning the pages of this book your heart will be moved by the beauty of trees. That you will occasionally think, 'wow.' That you will want to look at trees more closely yourself and become a dendrophil if you aren't one already.

– Ruthie Rosauer, Photographer and Tree Lover

"Look deep into nature, and then you will understand everything better." – Albert Einstein

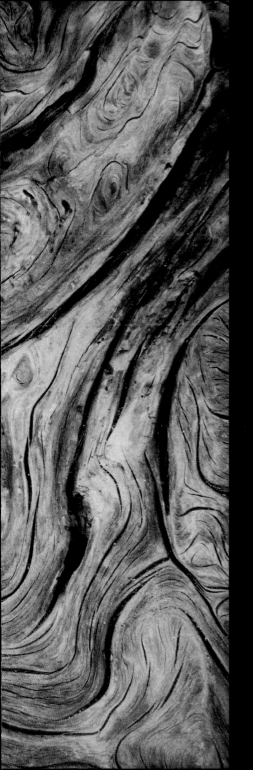

Bark

It is true that the bark of some trees is a pretty mundane surface of gray or brown or beige; but there are others that dazzle with their palettes and textures. Some, like the Lacebark Elm, create a miniature landscape of fissures and hills.

We are accustomed to seeing leaves change over the course of a year. But it surprises many to learn that, for most tree species, the bark will change its appearance dramatically as the tree ages. You will see this if you compare photos of a young black cherry's bark, to a mature specimen and then to an old veteran black cherry. Black spruce, Douglas fir and Eastern cottonwood are others with significant bark changes. This is one reason why trees can be so difficult to identify!

No Voice Inside

BY BARBARA QUICK

If we were oak trees, rooted to one place—
our movements too slow to perceive—
hikers along the trail would pause
and read our secret history
in the contortions caused
by obsolete impediments,
cleared, burned up or decomposed.
The relationships that made us grow
away from the sun, tortuously twisting
to find it again.
Lightning strikes that left us scarred and maimed.
Young loves' initials carved into our very skin—
as faint as the tracery of worms now.

No voice inside would wish for unmarked beauty
in place of such a silhouette against the sky.

Madroños

BY CARINE TOPAL

We saw them kneeling
burnished-barked
limbs shedding skin

curling from trunk
to branch where pale
green leaves led
to a flowering.

What seemed to be
spindled blossoms,
a cluster of celadon peas
the size of an infant's
fist, suspended
waiting for a kind pull from earth,

saw them balancing
beside another Manzanita
past its prime, which once
also blossomed
and pearled hopeful.

How even the damaged
and dying ones
stand bare, sun-
bleached to bone,
making us stop.

PAPERBARK MAPLE

BY SALLY ZAKARIYA

Wind animates the three-lobed leaves
curled to cup the summer air

A folio of bark peels off in shaggy sheets
scribbled with imagined verses

These paperbarks are artist trees
self-portraits *en plein air*

They tell their stories leaf by silent leaf
for us to read their changes

Fall brings a fiery palette, then winter
twigs write letters on the sky

In spring winged double seeds hang
glide on wind in artful acrobatics

Where they take hold another year
will bring its own new poetry

27

Singing My Song

by Ruthie Rosauer

I am a song of rain, tapping rhythms onto branches and leaves
Each note fragile, whipped by wind across lupine meadows.
Misting on towhee heads,
Each bird trilling 'give me drink, give me drink' oh Living Water!

I sing a song of blood, coursing through wolverine veins
Blood heavy with moon lust and fragrant forests.
Pulsing through coyote breast,
Each beast howling 'choose me, choose me' oh Opal Moon!

I sing a song of sap, of rivers rushing through phloem
Each ascending arpeggio a sugared tsunami.
Susserating through leaves of maple
Each tree whispering 'tap me, tap me' oh Beautiful One!

I am a song of water,
Of blood and sap and moon lust.
Whirling in the arms of my Beloved
I hurl crescendos at the sky and SING!

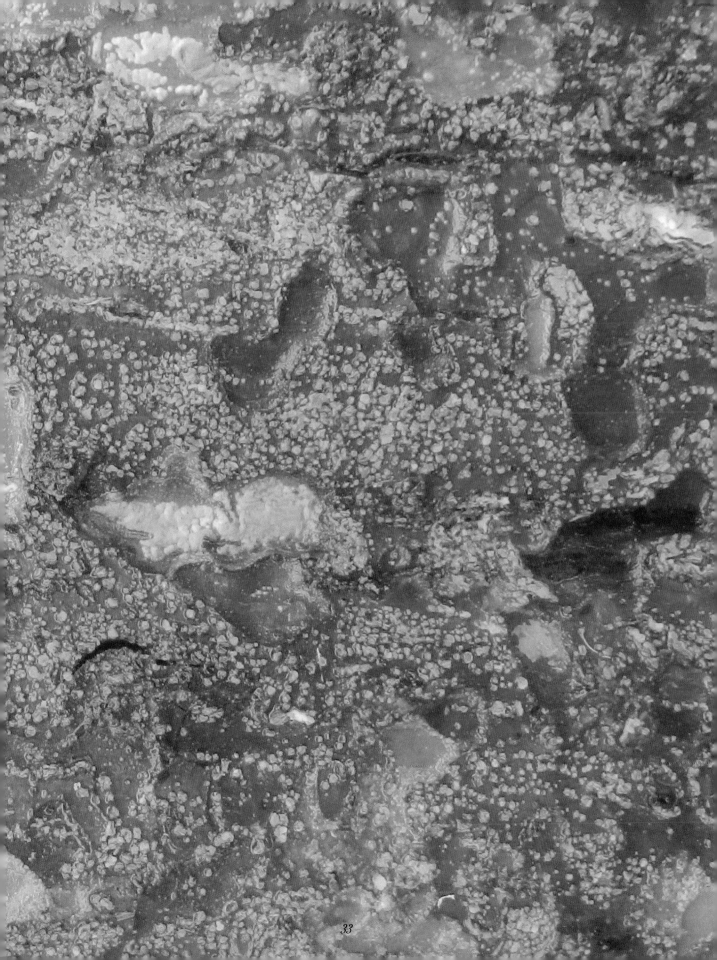

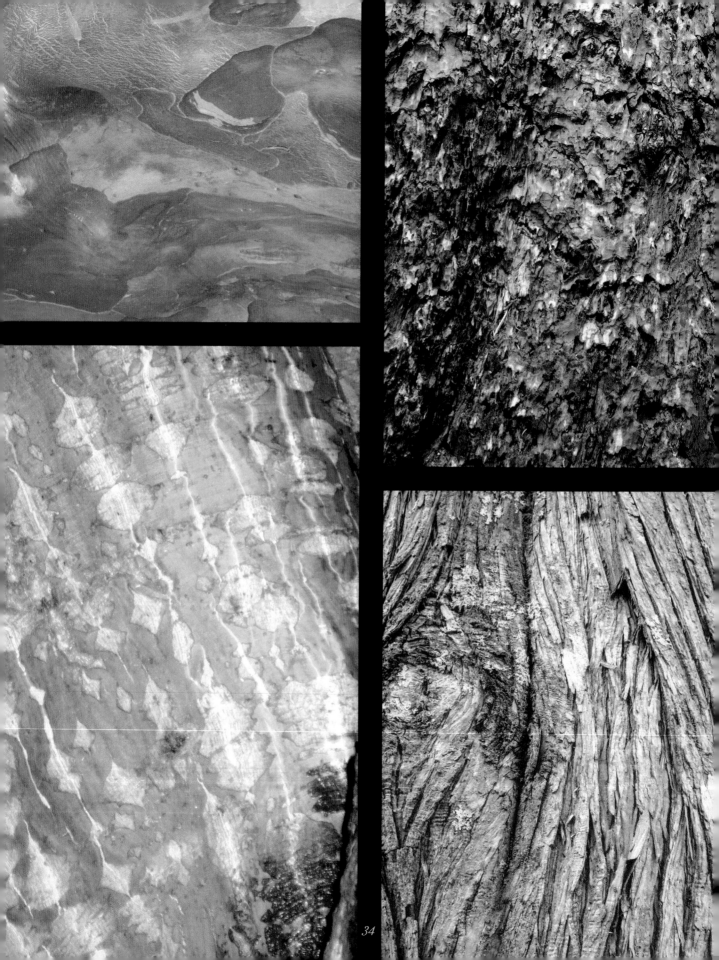

34

LEAVES

OF ALL THE PARTS OF A TREE, IT IS THE LEAVES THAT
MOST OFTEN CAPTURE OUR COLLECTIVE ATTENTION. LEAVES MAKE
PHILOSOPHERS WAX POETIC ABOUT THE 'SEASONS OF LIFE;' AND
POETS TURN PHILOSOPHICAL ABOUT THEIR CHANGING COLORS
AND EVENTUAL CRUMBLING INTO MULCH AND DUST.

IN TEMPERATE ZONES, LEAVES ARE A COLORFUL REMINDER OF
SEASONAL CHANGE. THEY ARE THE ROCKETTES OF THE ARBOREAL
WORLD. THEY DAZZLE AND DELIGHT, BECKON AND ENCHANT.
CARLOADS OF TOURISTS DRIVE THROUGH NEW ENGLAND,
THE OZARK MOUNTAINS AND THE BLUE RIDGE PARKWAY
TO OOH AND AAH OVER THEIR GLORY.

THE LEAVES OF DECIDUOUS TREES ARE EPHEMERAL. THE WORD,
'LEAVES,' IS ITSELF A CONSTANT REMINDER THAT THEY ARE WITH US
FOR ONLY A BRIEF TIME BEFORE THEY 'LEAVE' US!

INCLUDED IN THIS CHAPTER ARE EVERGREEN NEEDLES, WHICH
PERFORM THE SAME FUNCTIONS AS LEAVES – COLLECTING SUNLIGHT,
INTAKING CARBON DIOXIDE, AND 'EXHALING' OXYGEN. IN SOME
CLIMATES NEEDLES ARE SUPERIOR TO LEAVES IN THAT THEIR WAXY
COATING RETAINS MORE WATER, ARE MORE RESISTANT TO INSECTS
AND CAN SURVIVE ICE AND SNOW. IN MANY NORTHERN LOCATIONS
THEY ALSO PROVIDE WELCOME GREEN COLOR IN A WINTER
LANDSCAPE OF GRAY, BROWN AND WHITE.

When we tug at a single thing in nature, we find it attached to the rest of the world. – *John Muir*

MEMENTO MORI

BY KAREN SCHUBERT

I layer leaves into my
leaf bin. They are too
beautiful. Maybe that's why
I wonder about the old
tree, if it's long from
falling. The red leaves are
dying, leaving the sky
in their wake.

Yesterday

by Kenneth Weene

Yesterday summer still held to the branches;
This morning the leaves declare changes in the air.
Somewhere in Canada, shaggy moose collide;
The still wind of their might rushes southward
Changing the trees in one fast-moving night.
Soon the woods will walk with crackling sound
And earth will blanket herself against the cold.

Yesterday little children still ran about in shorts
And made believe that freedom had no end.
This morning their faces have taken on new cares
As they wait wrapped in warm sweaters
For yellow buses to grudgingly appear.
The parents clustered together against the chill
Don't laugh as much as yesterday they did.

Yesterday there seemed to be more birds
Scavenging the air and singing for our bread;
This morning the traffic noise has replaced them.
It is as cold as the northern wind.

*To sit in the shade on a fine day,
and look upon verdure is the most
perfect refreshment.*

— Jane Austen

Rain Meditation

by Robert Ratliff

Standing in the pouring rain,
shuddering as cold, wet drops
saturate our hair and drip
into our eyes and soak our shirts
and shorts and leak down filling up our shoes.

heart   beat
heart   beat

Breathing, gazing, at the pine
growing on the cold hill's side,
drenched from top to root like us
but never minding being soused.
You'd think it took delight in rainy days.

heart   beat
heart   beat

Suddenly, that great pine bent
our way and smiled and waved.
Then it laughed a cheery laugh
and we were laughing too.
Despite the whirling tempest gale,
it danced a blitheful, twirling mosh,
leading us from cloudburst to ecstasy.

Autumn's Legacy

by Juleigh Howard-Hobson

Earth tossed leaves are tan and broken,

Token

Each of last year's turning into fall.

All

Crushed and jumbled, cracked and jagged.

Ragged

Edges hide their forms. Elm? Oaken?

Woken

By an early springtime's breezy call,

Small

Swirls of leaf-dust dance up, avid –

Gravid

With energy of the life to come.

Some

Dress the flowers that they've guarded,

Yarded

Gardens rich with loam. Others fly, pall-

Mall

Random, to feed the planet, crumb-

By-crumb.

THE LEAVES OF AUTUMN

BY SARAH BROWN WEITZMAN

In Florida the seagrape's pingpongpaddle leaves
rust and drop in September and I remember
how in Port Washington my mother and I
collected October leaves, faded yellows,
dull burgundies and duns. Scarlets and
golds above my reach for I was seven.
"They, too," my mother said more to herself,
"will fall in time." She seemed so tired.

At home I pressed them between the pages
of an album. Pointy maples, sycamore fans,
catalpa hearts and jagged oaks. She spelled their names
so I could label them sumac, witch hazel, mulberry,
ash. But by the first snow when I opened those pages,
the leaves were brown crumbles of dust
and brought a stab of sadness I couldn't label

Tree Teachings

BY F. I. Goldhaber

Trees teach us
life lessons if we'll
listen: first
offer to
any who seek it shelter
and respite; second

spread your wealth
upon the ground to
share; third give
this planet
back more than you take; fourth breathe
life into the air.

CROWNING GLORIES

BUDS, FLOWERS, NUTS AND FRUITS APPEAR AS
THE MUCH-APPRECIATED PRODUCTS OF A TREE – THEIR
CROWNING GLORIES. AND YET THEY ARE ALL JUST PART OF
A TREE'S EVERYDAY EFFORT TO PROPAGATE ITSELF.

TREES ARE EITHER "GYMNOSPERMS" OR "ANGIOSPERMS"
DEPENDING ON WHETHER THEIR SEEDS ARE ON THE
OUTSIDE (GYMNOSPERM) OR ENCLOSED WITHIN A FRUIT
SUCH AS AN ACORN OR PAPAYA (ANGIOSPERM). TREES THAT
DON'T PRODUCE SEEDS ARE INCAPABLE OF REPRODUCING
ON THEIR OWN.

A TREE DOES NOT THINK, *I would like to produce
something beautiful today,* IT JUST DOES.

We plant seeds that will flower

as results in our lives, so best

to remove the weeds of anger, avarice,

envy and doubt, that peace and

abundance may manifest for all.

– Dorothy Day

DOGWOOD
BY F. I. GOLDHABER

Each spring I find the
cherry trees most beautiful
until dogwoods bloom.

Redbud

BY ANNELINDE METZNER

Still in April bare grey trees remind me that this is no dream,
this everyday, this every new day-
The cherry blossoms, first to bloom,
then scattering in breeze, reminding of snow,
and now today, lush and greener by the hour,
intent on producing sweet red fruit.

The hummer's return, a long, long drink,
fitting for one returned from Guatemala!
And then, *ecoutez!* Welcome the wood thrush,
her deep multilayered melody guiding me back.
Welcome thrush! Welcome me!
My eyes dilate, hummers buzz, and the chickadee not two feet from me,
cocking and cocking the wee head, seeming to want my finger for a perch.
A bluebird, shy as Spring's first new,
and cardinals, and goldfinch! A riot of color!
I can't translate this, I can't write it!

Along the banks of the river, redbud, misnamed in her purple gown,
paints filagrees in the forest canopy, here there and everywhere,
suspended in a perfect ballet, sucking my breath away.
The new dogwood, still clinging to green,
not yet ready for the full openness of total white.
I can't translate, I can't write.

Pale yellows and greens creep tenderly up the mountain,
a turkey buzzard gliding on the thermal winds.
A great peace relaxes me all along my spine,
up to my tippy-top, my eyes dilate, for the everyday of this,
it won't go away, tomorrow and tomorrow, hooray and hooray,
here's my world come back again, this day, this day, this very day.

For a seed to achieve its greatest expression, it must come completely undone. The shell cracks, its insides come out and everything changes. To someone who doesn't understand growth, it would look like complete destruction.

– Cynthia Occelli

Do not be afraid to go out on a limb... That's where the fruit is. – Anonymous

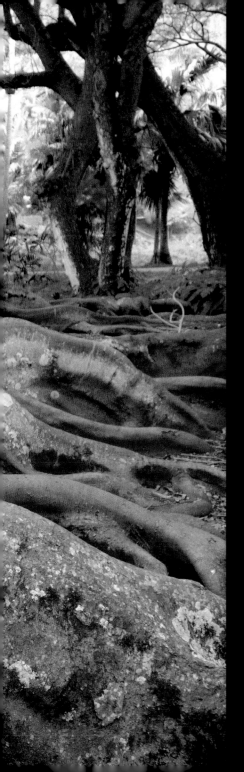

Roots

The word 'root' is used in many ways in English in addition to the obvious one of supplying nourishment to the rest of the tree. The root is the lowest note of a musical chord, the end of the tooth that connects it to the jaw and the end of a hair that connects it to the scalp. It is also used to define something as being essential to the core of something else (e.g. the root of all evil, family roots, roots of French cooking, roots of Bluegrass music). When we are checking on the health of a new venture we are reassured when told it is 'firmly rooted.'

The root of my own fascination with photographing trees lies with the roots of the Moreton Bay Fig trees I saw at the National Tropical Botanical Garden in Kauai. So 'three cheers' to tree roots – the unsung and often unseen heroes of the tree anatomy.

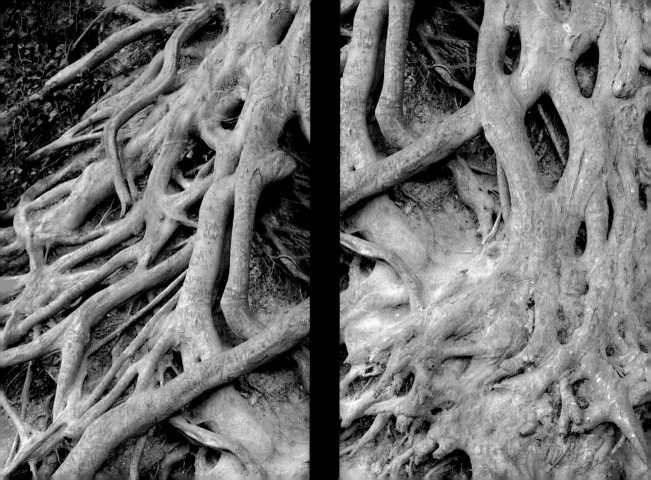

I Don't Want to be A Tree

BY LOIS MARIE HARROD

*"I don't want to be a tree,
I want to be its meaning."*
ORHAN PAMUK, *My Name Is Red*

I WANT TO BE THE GREENNESS OF THE LEAF
OPENING MYSELF TO WIND

TAKING IN THE MOLECULES THAT HAVE WARMED
THE LAMBS AND THE MICE

AND TURNING THEM AGAIN TO OXYGEN
THAT BREATH OF FIRE.

I WANT TO BE THE BLACK BRANCHES
SHINING IN THE DULL RAIN

THE WILD WATER SPLASHING
ON A BOY AND A GIRL STANDING AGAINST MY TRUNK.

I DON'T WANT TO BE A TREE,
I WANT TO BE ITS MEANING,

IN THE DEEP SEARCH FOR WATER
IN THE DIRT, THE ROOTS TONGUING

DOWN AND DOWN TO THE DARK PLACES
WHERE DEATH ABOUNDS.

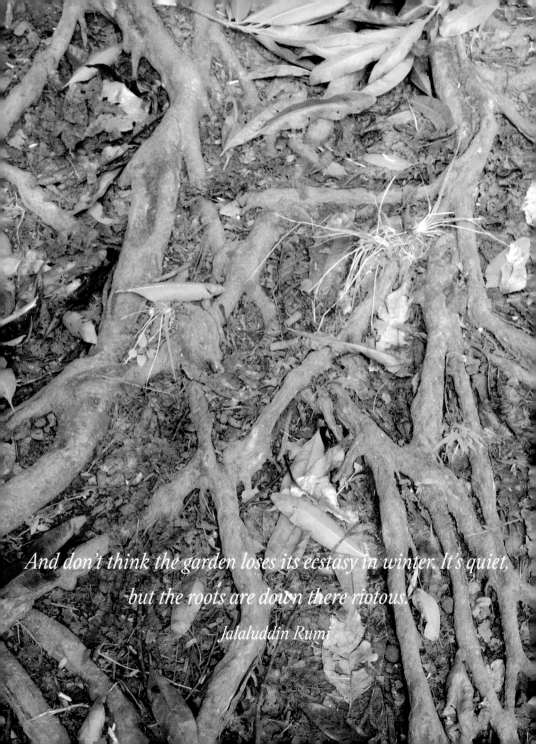

And don't think the garden loses its ecstasy in winter. It's quiet,
but the roots are down there riotous.

— *Jalaluddin Rumi*

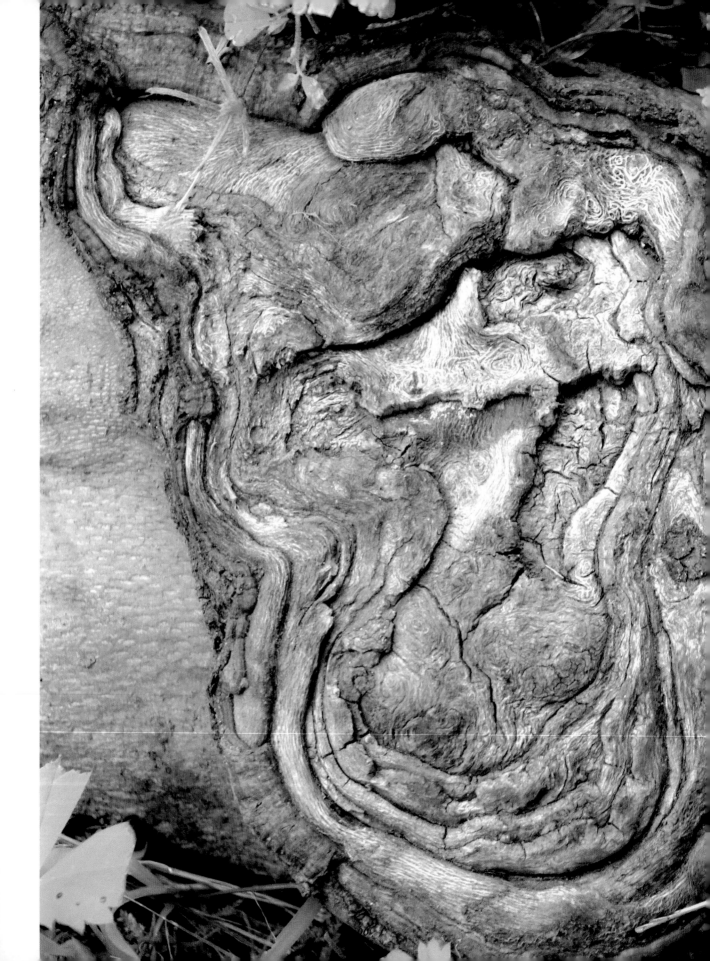

SHAPES

WE ARE IRRESISTIBLY DRAWN TO THE PRACTICE OF
ATTRIBUTING HUMAN FORM AND/OR PERSONALITY TRAITS
TO THINGS THAT ARE NOT HUMAN. DO YOU SEE A MOUTH
IN THE CHROME GRILLE OF AN ANTIQUE CAR? WINDOW
PANES THAT 'WINK' AT YOU? OR AN EYE IN THE BARK
OF A TREE? THIS TENDENCY TO ANTHROPOMORPHIZE IS
SPONTANEOUS AND HELPS US 'RELATE' TO NON-HUMAN
CREATURES AND OBJECTS.

MANY OF THE IMAGES IN THIS SECTION FOUND THEIR WAY
INTO THE 'SHAPES' SECTION BECAUSE OF THEIR SIMILARITY
TO AN 'EYE' OR A 'FACE.' OTHERS ARE INCLUDED BECAUSE
THEY HAVE FORMED ANOTHER INTERESTING DESIGN. YOU
MIGHT JUST LOSE YOUR HEART TO ONE OF THEM.

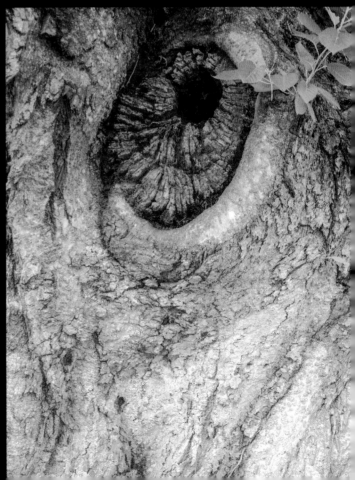

My True Loves

by Marilyn Sequoia

The trees are the only ones
Who ever really loved me.
I know, for in despair
I drove into the mountains where
I felt surrounded,
Bound in love by their presence.

Of me they asked nothing,
The mountain trees, save
Their right to flourish and grow.
They gentle me, those pines,
Peace me, calm me.
Slow me to beauty's pace,
Pull me tall,
Show me the sky,
Remind me of living.

And I descend
With my life again,
Thrilling to the curves
And the pinkened sunset
Of home.

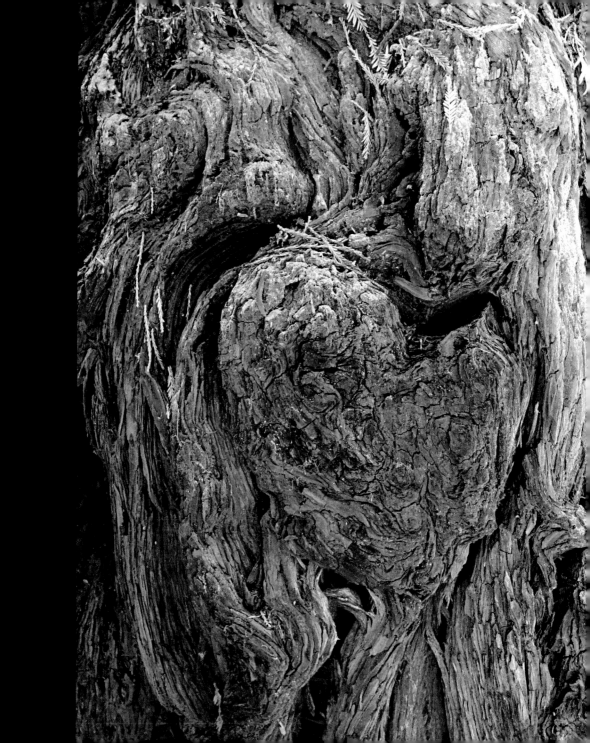

Holiness comes wrapped
in the ordinary.
There are burning bushes
all around you.
Every tree is full of angels.
Hidden beauty is waiting
in every crumb.

— Macrina Wiederkehr, O.S.B.

Tree branches

waving

smiling

pulling

whispering –

to me.

My friends...

My comfort...

My hope.

The strong trunks move

in the wind

but do not yield

until compelled by force.

Trees shelter

life

of all kinds,

in, near and around.

Human generations

a tree stands

sheltering all.

A tree is a world,

an island

on the prairie,

for shade.

A tree finds me

and I find...

a friend.

To The Woodland Wren

by Jean Cassidy

Alone
work
to survive
this short while.

Scrawny claws
scratch deadwood powder,
scatter sweet-sour peat
plunder the earth.

High above decay
dodge,
flit skyward
up and up no tether no bounds
until the tiniest branch becomes
your temporary rest.

You are, after all, only wind and feather
almost imperceptible,
weightless
thought.

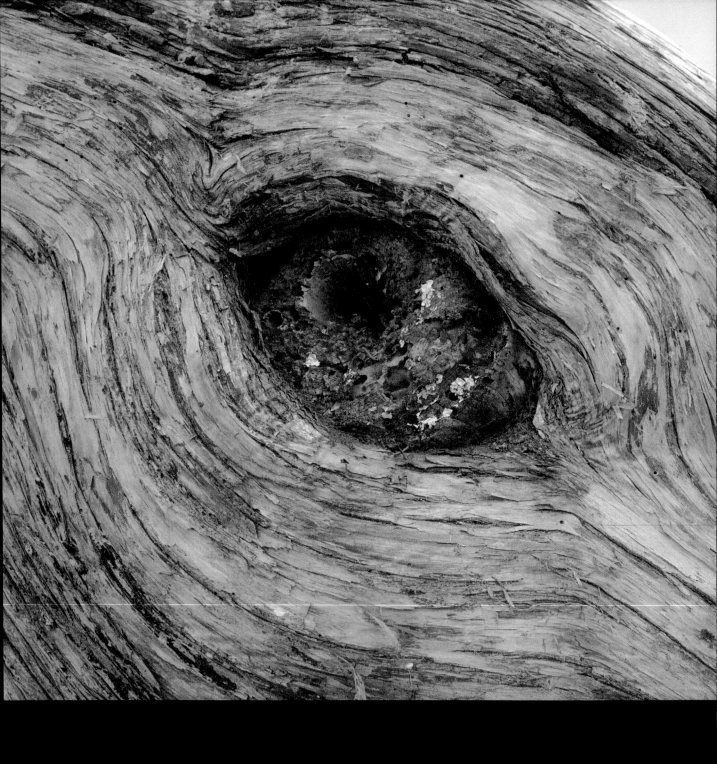

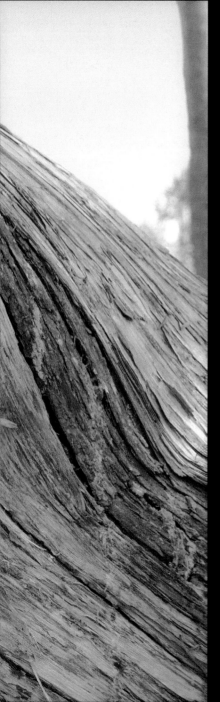

OLD TAPESTRY

BY ANNIE LIGHTHART

See how strong the thread is, how the tree of life is stitched into place,
how all your sad thought cannot dampen this cloth.

Someone has woven a trusted face into every branch.
Even the hungry roots bear that smiling gaze.

Nothing has been forgotten.
Within the branches, the flowers wear your eyes.
To look at even one petal is to see your life hidden everywhere.

Let yourself be silently drawn by
the strange pull of what you really love.
It will not lead you astray.

— Jalaluddin Rumi

One touch of nature makes the whole world kin.

– William Shakespeare

Whole Trees

Trees delight us with their small details: the texture of bark, the delicate appearance of a new leaf, the vein structure of a mature leaf, the winged samaras of maple trees that launch themselves into the wind and glide. But trees are equally glorious when viewed as a whole.

In this chapter, several trees were photographed solo – an independent statement of endurance and resiliency.

Other photos capture trees in groups because when we put several trees together into a collage of texture, shape and color – the effect can be breathtaking. This section features forests, manicured botanical gardens, half-wild arboretums, parks, residential yards and random clumps of trees by the side of the road.

The Hoh River and Rainforest
A Haiku Sequence

by SuzAnne C. Cole

colonnade of trees –
reminder of the nurse log
that once sustained them

Western red cedar –
coastal people called it
"the long life-maker"

deer wade glacier stream
maple flames on the far bank
autumn approaches

vast wings crack the sky
above gray snag's jagged crown –
ospreys feeding young

sun-dappled glade
female elk browses the tips
of saw-toothed sword fern

Green Cathedral

BY CAROL PEARCE BJORLIE

Watching these mountains,
waiting for saints to sing,
listening for their thin voices
to pierce the cloud-wreathed shroud,
I hear the hill's hidden heartbeat,
the lub-dub, lub-dub of the earth's core,
I stand beneath spruce spires, beech buttresses,
and gargoyles: eagle, owl, mountain cat.

The nave's silence
is broken by music of the Holy Muse,
hoo-hoo, caw, and scree;
the wind's scrape and sigh.
Every syllable is dear.

The lesson for the day is clear,
The lesson for the day is clear:
Persevere. Persevere.

Here – Autumn

by Carol Pearce Bjorlie

The trees are about to sing!
Show up for it.
Mile marker 365 on the Blue Ridge Parkway at sunset
will do.
The mountains are set to proclaim good tidings.

Which leaf libretto will the red orange gold brown
October singers choose to harmonize
as they stand on sloped risers in glory?

A roaring tribe in chaps, helmets, and skin sweep past,
Too loud, too quick, too lickety-split
to hear the score.

Tourists approach the drop off, "Ohh, Ahh!" pose/snap.
They exclaim over the choir in Russian, Punjabi, Arabic,
woven together at the cusp of Paradise.

I find myself using the words,
"Glory and gratitude."
"Glory and gratitude."

Delicious autumn! My very soul is wedded to it, and if I were a bird I would fly about the earth seeking the successive autumns.   – George Eliot

Tree Pose

by Barbara Quick

Yoga is practice for the exit—
the ecstatic drifting off in corpse pose, *shavasana*.
Vrikshasana: tree pose.

Roots growing down from the standing leg,
through the wooden floor, into the soil below.
One's aging skin covered in bark,
upward-reaching arms sprouting leaves,
hosting birds. Years measured in secret rings
with nothing at the center but the start.

The end of words and the longing
to make them sing. One's only sounds
a rote response to wind or rain
or ravening blade.

I am practicing now for my next life,
my wordless life, as a tree.
Holding my center tight,
sinking down while reaching toward the sky.
Gazing at something fixed
in my efforts not to wobble.
Feeling the chill of my naked foot
against my thigh.

The tree which moves some to tears of joy is in the
eyes of others only a green thing that stands in the way.
Some see nature all ridicule and deformity...
and some scarce see nature at all.
But to the eyes of the man of imagination,
nature is imagination itself.

– William Blake

A WALK IN THE WOODS

BY DIANE EGGE

Entering the woods,
trees part before me
like I'm royalty.
Branches form
a canopy overhead.
Fingers of sunlight peer through,
earthy incense of fallen leaves
permeates the air.

Spider webs of roots,
exposed by years of footsteps,
trip my feet.
Gray squirrels scamper
shopping for winter sustenance.
Soft needles hush my steps.
Winged friends make music.

The untroubled lake,
mirrors the hill of trees
splashed with fall colors.
Peace envelops me
like fog.
A bench near the water's edge
beckons me — come and sit.

My mind relaxes with my body.
Too soon I must
tear myself away
back to the world of concrete
and busyness.

Keep close to Nature's heart... and break clear away, once in awhile, and climb a mountain or spend a week in the woods. Wash your spirit clean.

– John Muir

For in the true nature of things, if we rightly consider, every green tree is far more glorious than if it were made of gold and silver.

– Martin Luther

ENTERING THE FOREST

BY CAROL DAVIS

You enter the forest
and it seals itself behind you.
How you find the opening
or where doesn't matter.
Only that you have crossed
an invisible threshold
and your previous life
vanishes imperceptibly
as if it were a snake
shedding, and you had missed
the moment when the old skin
becomes devoid of body and
the new one rustles down a foxhole.
All previous pain you have carried
with you, sewn carefully into secret
chambers, left behind.
The sun filters through the lace
of leaves scattering into dust
a thousand years old.
The giant mushrooms embrace you
with such tenderness no lover
could ever match.
With each step memory fades.
There is no turning back.
The stench of decay is the only
smell you have ever loved,
the moss your only bed,
this life the only one imaginable.

Nature does not hurry, yet everything is accomplished.

– Lao Tzu

CRONE OAK

BY KATE STOCKMAN

This majestic oak
Lifts embrittled arms to the sky
Full of laps moss-soft
    That cradle nests
    That protect babes
    That lull animals to rest.

Her arms stretch skyward
    To weather
    To accept
    To reach.

Even her head branches upwards
Into mighty, flowing tendrils
As gentle as Medusa's own,
    Offering shelter and shade,
    Dancing with the breezes,
    Antennae between earth and sky.

This magnificent oak has stood sentry
For over 150 years.
Now, she is dying
From greed:
    From roots choked with asphalt,
      A black-top grave;
    From butchering blades and saws,
      Wielded by blindness;
    From being
      Too regal
      Too old
      Too generous.

Soon, this exquisite Crone
Will be
   Cut apart
      Chopped down
         Split up.

Her limbs will whine
With chainsaw and chipper.
She will
   Tremble
      Bleed
         Cry
            Collapse.

The earth will shudder
   When she falls.
There will be a deep furrow
   Where she lies.
There will be a hole in the sky
   Where she reached.
There will be a soft mount in the earth
   Where she stood.

And she will be grievously missed.

Dialogue

by Carol Pearce Bjorlie

To those who love,
the mountains are not dumb:
sough, warble, hum
whoosh, rap, thrum.

Each mossy voice is understood
seasoned verbs from basalt and quartz
poems from venerable stream beds,
hoary lines on commitment from distant ridges,
the palaver of copper beech to rhododendron,
The oration of waterfalls!

The poet listening in these woods
Longs to translate their archaic tongue.

And suddenly you know: It's time to start something new
and trust the magic of beginnings.

– Meister Eckhart

ABOUT THE POETS

Bjorlie, Carol Pearce

"These Trees," "Dialogue," "Here Autumn,"
and "Green Cathedral"

Carol Pearce Bjorlie has two books of poetry
published, *Behind the Cello* by Main Street Rag,
Charlotte, NC and *Impossible Brightening* by
North Star Press, St. Joseph, MN. Her trilogy for
Young Adults, *Sweet Harmony*, was published by
Indigoseapress, NC. Carol lives in Asheville, NC.
Her motto: "I am not done yet!"

Cassidy, Jean

"To the Woodland Wren"
(First appeared in her book of poems, *Toward the
Clearing: poems with instrumental accompaniment*,
Main Street Rag, Charlotte, NC, 2014)

Jean Cassidy grew up in Chicago. She spent her
career developing and managing mental health
services delivery. Jean was a member of the
Dominican Sisters for 17 years. She is now manager
and co-owner of www.SheVille.org. She and her
spouse, Va Boyle, have lived in Asheville since 1996.

Cole, SuzAnne C.

"The Hoh River and Rainforest: A Haiku Sequence"
(First published as "The Hoh River and Rainforest:
A Haiku Sequence" in *Earth Blessings*, June Cotner,
ed., Viva Editions, 2016)

SuzAnne C. Cole, former college English instructor,
has been a featured poet at the Houston Poetry Fest
and won a Japanese haiku contest. Her poetry and
fiction have been nominated for Pushcart Prizes.
She also writes essays and plays.

Davis, Carol V.

"Entering the Forest"
(Won the Black Rock Press, Univ. of Nevada
Broadside Competition and was printed as a limited
edition broadside, 1995. Published in *It's Time to
Talk About . . .* Symposium, St. Petersburg,
Russia, 1997)

Carol V. Davis is author of *Because I Cannot Leave
This Body* (2017), *Between Storms* (2012) and
won the 2007 T.S. Eliot Prize for "Into the Arms of
Pushkin: Poems of St. Petersburg." She is poetry
editor of the Los Angeles *Jewish Journal*.

Egge, Diane

"A Walk in the Woods"

Diane Egge and her husband live in Cheyenne,
Wyoming, and travel extensively. She's previously
published poetry in *High Plains Register, Weather
Watch – Poems of Wyoming*, and the recently
released *Blood, Water, Wind and Stone* anthology.
www.dianeegge.com
Facebook: Diane Egge Author

Goldhaber, F.I.

"Dogwood" and "Tree Teachings"
("Dogwood" was first published on Twitter by Form.
Reborn and in a paper in *On A Narrow Windowsill*)

As a reporter, editor, and business writer, F.I.
Goldhaber produced articles, features, editorials,
and reviews for newspapers, corporations,
governments, and non-profits in five states. Now
her poetry, fiction, and essays appear in paper,
electronic and audio magazines, books and
anthologies. www.goldhaber.net

Harrod, Lois Marie

"I don't want to be a tree"
(First published in *The Ravens Perch:
Giving Breath to Words*
www.theravensperch.com/poetry/January 2016)

Lois Marie Harrod's 16th collection *Nightmares of
the Minor Poet* appeared in June 2016. *Fragments
from the Biography of Nemesis* and *How Marlene
Mae Longs for Truth*, in 2013. Widely published in
journals and online, she teaches Creative Writing at
TCNJ. Visit her website www.loismarieharrod.org

Herrmann, Duane L.

"Tree Friends"

Duane L. Herrmann is a survivor who lives on the
Kansas Prairie where he communes with trees in
the breeze and writes. He is published in print and
online, in this country and elsewhere. See also:
www.dlherrmann.wix.com/home or dlherrmann.
blogspot.com

Howard-Hobson, Juleigh

"Autumn's Legacy"

Juleigh Howard-Hobson's writing has appeared in
many places, including *The Lyric, Mezzo Cammin,
Verse Wisconsin*, and *The Raintown Review*. She
has been twice nominated for the Pushcart Prize.
Her fourth and most recent book is *Remind Me*
(Ancient Cypress Press).

Lighthart, Annie

"Old Tapestry"
(From *Iron String*, published by Airlie Press, 2013)

Annie Lighthart is a writer and teacher who started writing poetry after her first visit to an Oregon old-growth forest. Poems from her book *Iron String* have appeared on *The Writer's Almanac* and have traveled farther than she has.
www.annielighthart.com

Metzner, Annelinde

"Redbud"

Annelinde Metzner writes and composes for Mother Earth and the Divine Feminine. See new poems weekly at "Annelinde's World."
(www.annelindesworld.blogspot.com) She can be reached at annelinde@hotmail.com

Quick, Barbara

"No Voice Inside" and "Tree Pose"

Widely published novelist, poet and journalist Barbara Quick (www.BarbaraQuick.com) makes her home in the Wine Country of Northern California. Her much-loved 2007 novel from HarperCollins, *Vivaldi's Virgins*, has been translated into 15 languages.

Ratliff, Robert

"Rain Meditation"

Robert is a student of healing. He enjoys writing poetry, memoir, and fiction from his home in the mountains of North Carolina. His publications include "The Old Yellow Dog" in *Penumbra* and *The Bookmakers at Eden* on CreateSpace.

Schubert, Karen

"Memento Mori"

Karen Schubert's chapbooks include *Black Sand Beach* and *I Left My Wings on a Chair*. Her works appear in *Diode*, *Best American Poetry Blog*, *Waccamaw* and *PoetsArtists*. She is creative non-fiction editor for *Ragazine* and co-director of Lit Youngstown (LitYoungstown.org).

Sequoia, Marilyn

"My True Loves"
(By permission from *New Wilderness: Poems of Nature and of the City* / Talking Leaves Press 1997)

Marilyn Sequoia's love of trees began in Ohio, and blossomed amongst the redwoods of California. Marilyn's poems appear in her book *New Wilderness*, collections including *Discovering Spirit of Place*, UC Riverside's *Mosaic*, Habitat's *Raising the Roof*, plus Katya Williamson's *Bringing the Soul Back Home*.

Stockman, Kate

"Crone Oak"

Kate says this about herself:
I love words. I find irresistible their origins, their meanings, their similarities, their differences, even their appearance. I relish reading and crafting a well-written passage. I cherish playing with words and am passionate about puns. My epitaph will read, "She finally came to her wit's end."
www.KateStockmanDesigns.com

Topal, Carine

"Madroños"
(Published in *Malpais Review* in 2011)

Carine Topal has published four collections of poetry and teaches poetry and memoir in the Los Angeles and Palm Springs areas. She is the recipient of many poetry awards and writing residencies. Her website: www.carine-topal.com

Weene, Kenneth

"Yesterday"

Kenneth Weene writes novels, stories, essays, and poetry; all of which can be found at www.kennethweene.com

Weitzman, Sarah Brown

"The Leaves of Autumn"
(First published in *BLUELINE*, Vol. 33, 2012)

Sarah Brown Weitzman has had poems in hundreds of journals and anthologies including, *The New Ohio Review*, *The North American Review*, *Rattle*, *Mid-American Review*, *Poet Lore*, etc. Sarah received a National Endowment for the Arts Fellowship. Her fourth book, *Herman and the Ice Witch*, is a children's novel published by Main Street Rag.

Zakariya, Sally

"Paperbark Maple"

Sally Zakariya's poems have appeared in 50-some print and online journals. She is the author, most recently, of *When You Escape* (Five Oaks Press, 2016) and the editor of a poetry anthology, *Joys of the Table* (2015). Zakariya blogs at www.butdoesitrhyme.com.

ABOUT THE TREES

BARK

14-15
Name: Driftwood (unknown origin)
Location: California

16
Name: Erythrina Livingstonia
(aka "Aloe coral-tree")
Native: Africa
Location: McBryde Garden, Kauai, HI

17
Name: Monkeypod (aka "rain tree")
Native: Australia, South America and Asia
Location: National Tropical Botanical
Garden, Kauai, HI
Comment: Seed pods are edible

20-21
Name: Papaya (Carica)
Native: South and Central Americas
Location: Limahuli Garden, Kauai, HI
Comment: Papaya plants grow in three
sexes: male, female and hermaphrodite.

Name: Tulip Poplar
Native: Eastern North America
Location: Western North Carolina
Comment: Despite its name it is actually
part of the magnolia family.

23
Name: Madrone (aka "Arbutus")
Native: Coastal region of western
North America
Location: Oregon

24-25
Name: Paperbark Maple
Native: China
Location: Bullington Garden,
Hendersonville, NC

26-27
Name: Lacebark Elm
Native: Eastern Asia
Location: North Carolina Arboretum,
Asheville, NC

Name: Paperbark Melaleuca
Native: Australia, New Caledonia
and New Guinea
Location: Big Island, HI
Comment: The Hawaii Dept. of Natural
Resources classifies this tree as "most
invasive." Its pollen and sap can cause
rash and/or respiratory problems.

28-29
Name: Cork Oak
Native: SW Europe and NW Africa
Location: McConnell Garden, Redding, CA
Comment: Cork is harvested without
machines and without harming the tree for
making bottle stoppers and flooring.

Name: Lacebark Elm
Native: Eastern Asia
Location: Pennsylvania

Name: Live Oak
Native: North and South America, Europe
and Asia
Location: Jacksonville, FL

31
Name: Kamani
Native: Pacific and tropical Africa
Location: Limahuli Garden, Kauai, HI

32
Name: Lacebark Elm
Native: Eastern Asia
Location: NC Arboretum, Asheville, NC

34-35
Name: Crepe Myrtle
Native: China and Korea
Location: Charleston, SC
Comment: Crepe myrtles were first
introduced to Charleston, SC in 1790.

Name: Douglas Fir (old growth)
Native: Western North America
Location: Mt. Rainier National Park, WA

Name: Coast Redwood
Native: Central and northern
California coast
Location: California
Comment: The Coast Redwood is
technically a *Sequoia sempervirens*.
They are believed to be the world's
tallest trees.

Name: Red Vein Maple
Native: Japan
Location: Pennsylvania

Name: Plane tree
Native: Hybrid, probably hybridized
in London
Location: Pennsylvania

LEAVES

36-37
Name: Japanese Maple
Native: Japan, China, Korea, Mongolia
and Russia
Location: Pennsylvania

38-39
Name: Bigleaf Maple
Native: Western North America
Location: Hoh Rainforest, WA

Name: Gingko biloba
Native: China
Location: Wisconsin

42-43
Name: Birch
Native: North America, Asia and Europe
Location: Asheville, NC

46-47
Name: *Terminalia carolinesis*
(aka "Ka" tree)
Native: Micronesia
Location: McBryde Garden, Kauai, HI

Name: Breadfruit
Native: New Guinea
Location: McBryde Garden, Kauai, HI

49
Name: Autograph tree
Location: Paleaku Peace Garden,
Big Island, HI

50-51
Name: Bigleaf maple
Native: Western North America
Location: California

56
Name; Eastern Redbud
Native: Eastern North America
Location: Hendersonville, NC

CROWNING GLORIES

62-63
Name: Cherry
Native: Asia
Location: Hendersonville, NC

64-65
Name: Achiote
Native: Tropical America
Location: National Tropical Botanical
Garden, Kauai, HI
Comment: Used for food and
cosmetic coloring.

Name: Juniper
Native: Europe, SW Asia, North America
Location: Santa Fe, NM
Comment: Although it looks like a berry,
it is actually a seed cone. The ancient
Greeks used it for medicinal purposes.
It is widely used to flavor gin.

Name: Sterculia rubiginosa
Native: Southeast Asia
Location: National Tropical Botanical
Garden, Kauai, HI

Name: Kentucky Coffee Tree
Native: North America
Location: NC Arboretum, Asheville, NC
Comment: Although the roasted seeds
may be used as a coffee substitute, the
unroasted pods and seeds are toxic.

Name: Sea Putat (aka "Box Fruit"
or "Fish Poison")
Native: Islands of Indian and Pacific oceans
Location: Liliuokalani Garden,
Big Island, HI
Comment: All parts of this tree
are poisonous.

66-67
Name: Mgambo (aka "Zanzibar soapberry"
or "Hawaiian pussy willow")
Native: East Africa
Location: Paleaku Peace Garden, Big
Island, HI

68-69
Name: Papaya
Native: South and Central America
Location: McBryde Garden, Kauai, HI

Name: Hala
Native: Hawaii and Polynesia
Location: Limahuli Garden, Kauai, HI
Comment: Nicknamed "tourist pineapple"
because while on the tree the fruit
resembles a pineapple.

Name:Spondias dulcia (aka "Wi tree")
Native:Polynesia
Location: Paleaku Peace Garden,
Big Island, HI

Name: Baldcypress
Native: North America
Location: NC Arboretum, Asheville, NC
Comment: This deciduous conifer turns
brown or orange/brown in the fall before
dropping its needles. They can grow
for 600 years.

Name: Oranges
Native: Asia
Location: McBryde Garden, Kauai, HI

70-71
Name: Dogwood
Native: North America, Europe
Location: Hendersonville, NC

72
Name: Redbud
Native: North America
Location: Hendersonville, NC

74-75
Name: Cornus Capitata
(aka "Himalayan Strawberry Tree")
Native: India and China
Location: Humboldt Botanical Garden,
Eureka, CA

Name: Japanese maple samara
Native: Asia and Russia
Location: North Carolina
Comment: The 'samara' is the winged
seed pod of the tree.

76
Name: Moreton Bay Chestnut
Native: Australia
Location: Kauai, Hawaii
Comment: Leaves and seeds are toxic.

78-79
Name: Theobroma Cacao
Native: South America
Location: McBryde Garden, Kauai, HI

Name: Leatherleaf Mahonia
Native: China
Location: Hendersonville, NC

Name: Apples
Native: Central Asia
Location: Washington

80-81
Name: Magnolia 'Betty'
Native: Southeast Asia and
North America
Location: North Carolina Arboretum,
Asheville, NC

Name: Mimosa (a.k.a. "Silk tree")
Native: Middle East and Asia
Location: Kauai, HI

ROOTS

82-85
Name: Moreton Bay Fig
Native: Australia
Location: Allerton Garden, Kauai, HI

86-87
Name: Redwood
Native: North America, Europe and Asia
Location: Humboldt Redwoods State Park,
Weott, CA

88
Name: Eucalyptus
Native: Australia
Location: Kauai, HI

94-95
Name: Rudraksha (aka "Blue Marble Tree")
Native: East Asia
Location: Kauai, HI
Comment: Trees are said to have mystical
properties and have originated
from the tear drops of Lord Shiva.

96-97
Name: London Plane
Native: Hybridized most probably
in England
Where: Pennsylvania

98-99
Name: Banyan
Native: India
Location: Iraivan Hindu temple, Kauai, HI

SHAPES

100-101
Name: Sargent Weeping Hemlock
Location: North Carolina
Comment: First written references were to
seedlings found in the Fishkill Mountains
of New York in the 1800's. Tree named for
Henry Winthrop Sargent circa 1875.

105
Name: Redwood
Native: China, Europe and North America
Location: California

106-107
Name: Black Birch
Native: North America
Location: Blue Ridge Parkway, NC

108-109
Name: Japanese White Pine
Native: Japan
Location: Pennsylvania

Name: Blue Atlas Cedar
Native: Morocco and Algeria
Location: Pennsylvania

Name: Japanese Maple
Native: Asia and Russia
Location: Hendersonville, NC

110-111
Name: Live Oak
Native: Southeastern U.S.A.
Location: Houston, TX

114-115
Name: Ironwood
Location: Kealia Beach, Kauai, HI
Comment: Many types of trees are
called 'ironwood' in their own local area.
This tree was identified to me as
'ironwood' by three reputable sources,
which is why I use it here.

116-117
Name: Cypress
Native: Pangea (the supercontinent that
existed more than 150 million years ago)
Location: Kingsley Plantation,
Jacksonville, FL

118-119
Name: Mountain Laurel
Native: North America
Location: North Carolina Arboretum,
Asheville, NC

WHOLE TREES

126-127
Location: Palmer Chapel, Cataloochee Valley, Great Smoky Mountains National Park, NC

128-129
Name: Japanese Flowering Crab
Native: Japan and East Asia
Location: Pennsylvania

130-131
Name: Nurse log
Location: Olympic National Park, WA

132-133
Name: Redbud
Native: North America
Location: North Carolina Arboretum, Asheville, NC

136-137
Location: Blue Ridge Parkway, NC

140
Name: Monkeypod
Native: Australia
Location: Allerton Garden, Kauai, HI

142-143
Name: Monkeypod
Native: Australia
Location: Big Island, near Naalehu, HI

144-145
Name: Alder
Native: Europe, North and South America
Location: Fern Canyon, Prairie Creek Redwoods State Park, California

146-147
Location: Blue Ridge Parkway, NC

148-149
Location: Kuilau Ridge trail, Kauai, HI
Comment: View of Mount Wai'ale'ale

150-151
Location: Kealia Beach, Kauai, HI

152-153
Location: Kephart Prong trail, Great Smoky Mountains National Park, NC

154-155
Name: Beech
Native: Europe, Asia and North America
Location: North Carolina

Name: Katsura
Native: Japan
Location: Pennsylvania

160-161
Name: Live Oak
Native: North and South America, Europe and Asia
Location: Jacksonville Arboretum, Jacksonville, FL

162
Name: Beech
Native: Europe, Asia and North America
Location: North Carolina

164-165
Location: Glacier National Park, MT

166-167
Location: Crooked Creek, Hendersonville, NC

Suggestions for Further Exploration

Books:

Blackwell, Lewis. (2009). *The Life & Love of Trees.*
San Francisco: Chronicle Books.

This book is a work of art.

Hugo, Nancy Ross. (2011). *Seeing Trees Discover the Extraordinary Secrets of Everyday Trees.*
Portland: Timber Press.

Hugo wants people to look more closely at trees in their local environment. Ten types of trees were chosen as the subjects for this work. Although this book is a bit heavy on text, photographer Robert Llewellyn did a superb job of photography.

Jahren, Hope. (2016) *Lab Girl.*
New York: Alfred A. Knopf

Primarily a narrative of a female who becomes a research scientist and the difficulties she encounters due to her gender. As an ecologist she looks at the 'big picture' but woven within this narrative are some interesting insights about trees.

Kingsbury, Noel. (2014). *The Glory of the Tree An Illustrated History.*
Buffalo: Firefly Books.

This book contains exceptionally beautiful photographs of 91 species of trees. Text about botany and tree origins accompany each photograph.

Kirk, Ruth and Jerry Franklin. (1992). *The Olympic Rainforest An Ecological Web.*
Seattle: University of Washington Press.

Good for information specifically about the Olympic rain forest.

Lewington, Anna and Edward Parker. (1999). *Ancient Trees: Trees that live for a thousand years.*
London: Collins & Brown.

If you want to know which trees can and do live to be a thousand years old then this is a good resource guide.

Moon, Beth. (2014). *Ancient Trees Portraits of Time.*
New York: Abbeville Press.

Photographer Beth Moon used a Pentax 6.7 film camera to capture images of trees. Her platinum/palladium printing technique makes for a visual feast in black, white and gray.

Pakenham, Thomas. (1999). *Meetings with Remarkable Trees.*
New York: Random House.

This book offers a unique historical perspective and pedigree to very specific trees with documentation in local lore and literature.

Preston, Richard. (2007). *The Wild Trees.*
New York: Random House.

If you can get past the first few chapters, you will be excited by the discoveries made by amateurs and scientists who explore the habitats generated in the highest redwood tree tops.

Rodd, Tony and Jennifer Stackhouse. (2008). *Trees A Visual Guide.* Los Angeles: University of California Press.

Includes fabulous color photographs, information about trees and related topics. A section entitled, "Remarkable trees of the world," is a guide to 99 of 'the world's most exceptional trees' including the frankincense tree and the horseradish tree.

Tudge, Colin. (2007). *The Tree: A Natural History of What Trees Are, How They Live and Why They Matter.*
New York: Crown Publishers.

This book has no photographs, but does include some lovely black and white hand drawings of trees. It provides heavily detailed information on the taxonomy and evolution of trees.

Wojtech, Michael. (2011). *Bark: A Field Guide to Trees of the Northeast.*
Hanover and London: University Press of New England.

Provides in-depth instruction on identification of trees based on their bark. Informational field guide includes line drawings and photographs.

Articles:

Pietowski, Alex. November 21, 2016 "Not Just Bees, Trees are dying off at an alarming rate with little public attention." *Waking Times.*

Reynolds, Gretchen. March 17, 2016. "Greenery (or Even Photos of Trees) Can Make Us Happier." *The New York Times*

Places to visit trees:

What better way to extend your study and adoration of trees than to visit them up close and in person? I have visited each of the following places and can guarantee you will find at least a dozen trees that will fascinate you.

Brookgreen Gardens –
Murrells Inlet, South Carolina

Bullington Gardens –
Hendersonville, North Carolina

Daniel Stowe Botanical Garden
Charlotte, North Carolina

Great Smoky Mountains National Park –
Cherokee, North Carolina

Hoh Rainforest, Olympic National Park –
Forks, Washington

Humboldt Botanical Gardens –
Eureka, California

Jacksonville Arboretum –
Jacksonville, Florida

Jedidiah Smith State Park –
Crescent City, California

Longwood Gardens –
Kennett Square, Pennsylvania

McConnell Arboretum –
Redding, California

Middleton Place –
Charleston, South Carolina

Morris Arboretum –
Philadelphia, Pennsylvania

National Tropical Botanical Gardens
(Allerton and McBryde) – Kauai, Hawaii

North Carolina Arboretum –
Asheville, North Carolina

Santa Fe Botanical Garden –
Santa Fe, New Mexico

Tyler Arboretum –
Media, Pennsylvania

Winterthur Garden –
Winterthur, Delaware

Acknowledgements

I would like to thank several people who have encouraged my photography explorations. In no particular order they are: Aviva Kahn, Jean Tuech, Nancy Ramp, Nancy Imhof, Marilyn Hubbard, Patricia Minard, Don and Diane Emon, Thomas and Andrea Gray, Richard and Bess Serr and Larry and Marie Past.

I deeply appreciate the time and effort made by Dick Bury, Allen Graham, Jonathan Gross and staff of the National Tropical Botanical Gardens for plant identification. All errors are strictly my own.

Thank you to Liz Hill and Virginia Bielski for encouraging me every step of the way and accompanying me for many hours while I took pictures.

THE END